PowerKiDS
Readers
MY COMMUNITY
MI COMUNIDAD

# A TRIP TO THE GROCERY STORE

---

# DE VISITA EN LA TIENDA

Josie Keogh

Traducción al español: Eduardo Alamán

**PowerKiDS**
press™

New York

Published in 2013 by The Rosen Publishing Group, Inc.
29 East 21st Street, New York, NY 10010

First Edition

Editor: Amelie von Zumbusch
Book Design: Ashley Drago

Traducción al español: Eduardo Alamán

Photo Credits: Cover, p. 23 Shutterstock.com; p. 5 Peter Dazeley/Riser/Getty Images; pp. 6, 9 Hemera/Thinkstock; p. 11 Ed Lallo/Photolibrary/Getty Images; p. 12 Noel Hendrickson/Digital Vision/Thinkstock; p. 15 Andersen Ross/Iconica/Getty Images; p. 16 Taxi/Getty Images; p. 19 iStockphoto/Thinkstock; p. 20 Photodisc/Thinkstock.

Library of Congress Cataloging-in-Publication Data

Keogh, Josie.
  [Trip to the grocery store. English & Spanish]
  A trip to the grocery store = De visita en la tienda / by Josie Keogh; [translated by Eduardo Alamán]. — 1st ed.
    p. cm. — (Powerkids readers: my community / Mi comunidad)
  Includes index.
  ISBN 978-1-4488-7827-7 (library binding)
  1. Supermarkets—Juvenile literature. 2. Grocery shopping—Juvenile literature. I. Title. II. Title: Visita en la tienda.
  HF5469.K4618 2013
  381'.456413–dc23
                                                2011049995

Websites: Due to the changing nature of Internet links, PowerKids Press has developed an online list of websites related to the subject of this book. This site is updated regularly. Please use this link to access the list:
www.powerkidslinks.com/pkrc/groc/

Manufactured in the United States of America

CPSIA Compliance Information: Batch #CS12PK: For Further Information contact Rosen Publishing, New York, New York at 1-800-237-9932

# CONTENTS

# CONTENIDO

The grocery store sells food.

La tienda vende alimentos.

There are many kids there.

---

Hay muchos chicos en
la tienda.

7

Jess gets food for lunch.

Jess compra comida para su almuerzo.

Daniel picks out fruit.

_____

Daniel elige fruta.

RED
DELICIOUS
$1.19
LB

11

VALLEY PRIDE
12
1%
MILK 4 Litres

Sam finds milk!

---

¡Sam encuentra la leche!

13

Jack gets meat for dinner.

---

Jack elige la carne para la cena.

The label says what is in a food.

Las etiquetas nos dicen qué hay en los alimentos.

17

Miguel likes rye bread.

A Miguel le gusta mucho el pan de centeno.

19

20

You pay right before you leave.

---

Antes de salir de la tienda,
hay que pagar.

Jane carries a big bag home.

---

Jane se lleva una bolsa grande a casa.

# WORDS TO KNOW / PALABRAS QUE DEBES SABER

**cashier**: A person people give money to.

**cajera (o)**: Persona a la que le damos dinero.

**dairy**: Having to do with milk.

**productos lácteos**: Que vienen de la leche.

**deli counter**: A place that sells cold meats.

**charcutería**: donde se venden fiambres.

## INDEX

## ÍNDICE